London Hughes

Biography Of a British Comedian and Television presenter

Chronicle Crafters

TABLE OF CONTENTS

INTRODUCTION

In the realm of comedy, where humor reigns supreme and laughter knows no borders, there exists a brilliant star, a force of nature, and a pioneer who has taken the stage by storm. Her name is London Hughes and her path through life has been nothing short of miraculous.

Born on September 7, 1989, in the bustling borough of Thamesmead in southeast London, England, London Hughes entered this world with a spark that would one day set the comedy scene ablaze. While her early years may have happened in the comparatively humble surroundings of

Thamesmead, they created the framework for a spectacular journey to comedy success.

London's narrative is one of persistence, determination, and a tireless pursuit of her aspirations. Raised in a single-parent family by her mother, a committed nurse, she acquired the principles of hard work and tenacity from an early age. It was her mother's unflinching support and undying affection that created the base around which London would build her future achievements.

From an early age, it was apparent that London Hughes exhibited a talent for acting that was nothing short of mesmerizing. Even in her earliest years, she demonstrated a natural tendency to amuse, frequently putting on spontaneous events for her family and friends. It was here, in the warm living rooms and little gatherings of Thamesmead, that the roots of her hilarious brilliance were planted.

As London Hughes entered puberty, she set her eyes on a challenging goal: to pursue her love for the performing arts. This goal brought her to the famed halls of the Brit School for Performing Arts and Technology in Croydon. Within those hallowed halls, she refined her abilities and cultivated the skills that would eventually become her comic arsenal.

Upon graduating from the Brit School, London Hughes went on a career that would take her from the tiny stages of local clubs and pubs to the huge stadiums of international comedy festivals. It was in these modest beginnings that she found her passion for stand-up comedy, equipped with nothing but her wit, charm, and an unyielding drive to make the world laugh.

In 2009, London's fame started its ascension when she joyfully won victory in the Laughing Horse New Act of the Year competition. This important event acted as the launch pad for her career, thrusting her into the limelight of the comedy world. It was a win that signified the entrance of a new, brave, and savagely humorous voice in the business.

London Hughes's early attempts into television displayed her flexibility as a performer. She graced the screens of famous programs such as The Bill, Casualty, and Holby City, showcasing her ability to smoothly switch between the tragic and humorous worlds. However, it was her breakthrough appearance in the BBC Three comedy series **Laughter Shock** in 2014 that confirmed her place as a rising star in the comic galaxy.

Laughter Shock was a surprise. A sketch comedy program that openly explored contentious subjects like race, gender, and sexuality, it offered a platform for London Hughes to flourish. Her performances were riveting, filled with energy, humor, and a brazen contempt for limits. Audiences and reviewers alike were charmed by her distinctive style of comedy, which mixed smart social critique with shameless frivolity.

Yet, London Hughes's adventure did not finish there. Her journey into cinema featured appearances in movies like **It's a Lot** (2013) and **The Comedian's Guide to Survival** (2016), further solidifying her image as a versatile performer.

Her presence on the radio was equally engaging. London Hughes became a radio personality, gracing stations such as Capital Xtra and BBC Radio 1Xtra with her engaging and lively approach. She proved that her abilities transcended the visual medium, making her a powerful force in the aural sphere as well.

In 2017, London Hughes reached a huge milestone when she got the Amused Moose Comedy Award at the Edinburgh Fringe Festival for her play **To Catch a Dick**. This distinction was a testimonial to her humorous talent and the tenacious spirit that characterizes her path.

Beyond her job, London Hughes is a light of generosity and activism. She has generously donated her time and energy to philanthropic organizations, including Stand Up to Cancer and Comic Relief. Moreover, she has utilized her position to bring attention to the need for mental health awareness, speaking frankly about her issues with anxiety and despair.

As we dive further into the pages of this biography, we shall learn the subtleties of London Hughes's life and work. We will examine the humor, the obstacles, the successes, and the tenacious spirit that have made her a comic legend.

In the realm of comedy, where a well-timed punchline can transcend frontiers and connect hearts, London Hughes stands as a monument to the lasting power of humor and the unlimited potential of a distinctive comic voice.

CHAPTER 1

Early Life and Family Background

London Hughes, the popular British comedian and performer, was born on September 7, 1989, in Thamesmead, a borough located in the southeast of London, England. Thamesmead, recognized for its varied culture and unusual architecture, served as the background for London's early existence.

London was reared in a single-parent family, with her mother having a significant part in her development. Her mother, a nurse, became not only her carer but also her inspiration and role model. London frequently considers her mother as her "hero" owing to the consistent support and direction she offered during her early years. From an early age, London Hughes learned the principles of hard work and independence, characteristics that would be vital in her quest for success.

During her youth, London displayed a particular interest in performing and entertaining people. She would regularly put on spontaneous acts for her family and friends, exhibiting her innate talent to make people laugh. This early predilection for humor and entertainment was a portent of things to come.

As she approached her teenage years, London's interest in the performing arts prompted her to join the Brit School for Performing Arts and Technology in Croydon. This prominent school gave her a formal education in theater and refined her talents as a performer. The experience at the Brit School surely had a key part in molding her creative skills preparing her for the tough world of entertainment.

Upon graduating from the Brit School, London Hughes lost little time in pursuing her goal of being a comedian. She began on her stand-up comedy adventure, making performances at small clubs and pubs in London. Her humorous ability started to flourish, gaining her fame and a growing fan following within the comedy industry.

In 2009, London accomplished a key milestone in her career when she was chosen to compete in the Laughing Horse New Act of the Year competition. Not only did she participate, but she emerged as the champion of the tournament. This triumph was a turning point in her career, opening doors to possibilities she had only dreamt about.

London Hughes's victory in the Laughing Horse competition opened the path for her to perform on different television programs, further confirming her image as a budding comedy sensation. Her sharp humor and charismatic presence made her a sought-after guest on prominent shows including The Russell Howard Hour, 8 Out of 10 Cats, and Mock the Week.

Despite her future accomplishments, London's early existence was not without its hardships. In a forthright 2018 interview with The Guardian, she disclosed that she had suffered homelessness for a spell after leaving home at the age of 18. This tragedy only fuelled her resolve to fulfill her ambitions in the entertainment business, exhibiting her tenacity and uncompromising devotion to her work.

In conclusion, London Hughes's early childhood was distinguished by her enthusiasm for performing, the impact of her committed mother, and her indomitable spirit. Growing up in Thamesmead and attending the Brit School gave her the grounding she needed to pursue a comedy career.

Her path from tiny comedy clubs to winning renowned contests and starring on television displays her skill and ambition to make her mark in the world of entertainment. London Hughes's incredible tale continues to inspire budding comedians and acts as a tribute to the power of tenacity and self-belief.

CHAPTER 2

Career Beginnings

London Hughes's path into the world of comedy and entertainment is a fascinating story of skill, persistence, and perseverance. Her career took off following her graduation from the elite Brit School for Performing Arts and Technology in Croydon, where she polished her abilities in theater.

Following her stint at the Brit School, London Hughes went on a road that would ultimately bring her to comic success. She started doing stand-up comedy at local clubs and pubs, where she refined her skill and rapidly acquired acclaim for her sharp wit and fascinating stage presence.

In 2009, London scored a key milestone in her career by winning the Laughing Horse New Act of the Year competition. This triumph was a turning point and provided her with a platform to demonstrate her comic abilities on a broader stage. It was a testimonial to her comic talent and the distinctive voice she brought to the comedy industry.

London Hughes's early journey into television includes appearances on prominent programs including The Bill, Casualty, and Holby City. Her flexibility as a performer was obvious as she delved into many professions within the entertainment business. Notably, she acted as a presenter on the adult chat channel Babestation, using the alias "Miss London."

In 2012, London moved her talent to the radio waves, creating and acting in her own BBC Radio 4 comedy pilot, 28 Dates Later. The program took inspiration from her personal experiences with online dating and gave her a forum for her to exhibit her comic writing abilities.

However, it was in 2014 that London Hughes had her breakout moment when she developed and acted in the BBC Three comedy series Laughter Shock. The presentation resonated with fans and reviewers alike, establishing her as a rising star in the world of comedy.

Her ability for comedy, along with her charming personality, made her a sought-after guest on prominent television series such as 8 Out of 10 Cats, Mock the Week, and The Russell Howard Hour.

Beyond television, London Hughes took her abilities to the silver screen with performances in films like It's a Lot (2013) and The Comedian's Guide to Survival (2016). Her ability to adapt fluidly across numerous types of media demonstrated her versatility as a performer.

In addition to her television and film work, London Hughes has created a reputation for herself as a radio host on stations like Capital Xtra and BBC Radio 1Xtra, further confirming her image as a multidimensional personality in the entertainment world.

London Hughes's accomplishment in comedy has not gone unnoticed, as she has received multiple distinctions during her career. In 2017, she got the Amused Moose Comedy Award at the Edinburgh Fringe Festival for her play To Catch a Dick, cementing her standing as a comic force to be reckoned with. She has also been nominated for numerous prizes, including the Chortle Award for Best Breakthrough Act and the Funny Women Award.

CHAPTER 3

Breakthrough with Laughter Shock

London Hughes's career-defining moment happened in 2014 when she created and acted in the BBC Three comedy series **Laughter Shock**. This sketch comedy presentation not only attracted viewers but also confirmed her place as an emerging star in the world of comedy.

Laughter Shock was a breakthrough program that starred London Hughes with a superb ensemble cast of comedians. Together, they produced a diversified mix of skits and sketches that encompassed a wide spectrum of issues. What set the program different was its fearlessness in confronting contentious and thought-provoking subjects, including race, gender, and sexuality. The series bravely dug into these difficult themes with a distinct combination of comedy, wit, and irreverence.

London Hughes's contribution to **Laughter Shock** was nothing short of spectacular. Her performances on the program were distinguished by unbounded energy, incisive wit, and an uncompromising approach to humor. Audiences and reviewers alike were captivated by her particular approach, which flawlessly blended smart social critique with uncontrolled hilarity. This brilliant mix displayed her comic talent and positioned her as a leader in the world of comedy.

Laughter Shock wasn't simply a performance; it was a platform that enabled London Hughes to demonstrate her ability, unique viewpoint, and willingness to approach tough themes via comedy. Her work on the series gained her a reputation for pushing the limits of humor while retaining a deep sense of sensitivity and tolerance.

In addition to her starring role in Laughter Shock, London Hughes continues to create waves in the comedy industry with her stand-up performances and appearances on numerous television series. Her ability to approach hard themes with comedy and empathy resonated with audiences, making her not just a comic but also a role model for budding comedians worldwide.

Throughout her career, London Hughes has won well-deserved awards and recognition for her contributions to comedy. In 2017, she got the renowned **Amused Moose Comedy Award** at the Edinburgh Fringe Festival for her play **To Catch a Dick**, further establishing her standing as a comic force to be reckoned with. Her talents have also led to nominations for respected accolades such as the **Chortle Award for Best Breakthrough Act** and the **Funny Women Award**.

In conclusion, London Hughes's breakout moment with **Laughter Shock** in 2014 was a turning point in her career, establishing her as a rising star in the comedy industry. Her ability to approach tough and contentious themes with comedy and intellect, as displayed on the program, marked her apart as a comic of great skill and insight. Since then, London Hughes has continued to make a huge influence in the comic business, garnering honors and influencing comedians worldwide with her distinct style of humor and daring approach to comedy.

CHAPTER 4

Television Career

London Hughes has proved her ability as a performer by working on a range of television series during her career. Notably, she started her adventure as a presenter on the adult chat channel Babestation, assuming the alias of "Miss London." She has admitted that this event was a fantastic learning opportunity that considerably helped her grow as a performer.

In addition to her job on Babestation, Hughes has made multiple appearances on CBBC, the children's programming division of the BBC. Her contributions include participation in programs such as The Dog Ate My Homework, Hacker Time, and Sam & Mark's Big Friday Wind-Up. These visits enabled her to interact with a younger audience while offering her brand of comedy.

In 2015, London Hughes was featured in a memorable episode of the long-running children's program Blue Peter. During her tenure on the show, she took on the role of an educator, teaching viewers how to produce their comedic videos—an experience that blended pleasure with knowledge.

Further displaying her flexibility, Hughes has been featured on many seasons of the CBBC travel program All Over the Place. In this series, she and colleagues presenters travel on excursions to varied areas throughout the globe, looking into local culture and traditions. Her engagement in this program showcased her capacity to discover and understand the world's variety.

Since 2016, London Hughes has earned a regular presenting role on the Saturday morning children's program Scrambled! This lively program mixes games, music, and comedic skits, gaining accolades for its colorful energy and ingenuity. Her continuous appearance on Scrambled! enhances her relationship with younger fans.

In addition to her work in children's programming, Hughes has made prominent appearances on various television series, including 8 Out of 10 Cats, Mock the Week, and The Russell Howard Hour. These performances in adult-oriented comedic contexts further highlight her flexibility as a performer.

Collectively, London Hughes's considerable work on television has not only displayed her flexibility but also helped establish her as a multifaceted entertainer with a unique voice and viewpoint. Her ability to captivate audiences of all ages and her devotion to pushing the limits of humor has secured her place as a vibrant presence in the world of entertainment.

CHAPTER 5

Film and Radio Work

London Hughes has expanded her influence beyond television, having a considerable effect in the areas of cinema and radio. These different projects have further proved her adaptability and creative brilliance.

In 2013, London Hughes entered the British comedy film scene with her performance in **It's a Lot**, directed by Femi Oyeniran. The film centers on the journey of Shaun, a young budding rapper, and London Hughes plays the part of Shaun's lover, Shanice. Her performance drew accolades from viewers and critics alike, displaying her ability to add depth and dimension to her on-screen performances.

Apart from her triumphs in movies, Hughes has made her stamp on the radio waves. In 2012, she demonstrated her abilities as both a writer and actor by crafting her own BBC Radio 4 comedy pilot, **28 Dates Later**. This comedy, inspired by her personal experiences with internet dating, connected strongly with fans and critics. It not only verified her position as a great writer but also showed her ability to generate material that captivates and entertains.

London Hughes has also stepped into the area of radio presenting, where she has made a huge impression. Her engaging and amusing attitude has made her a prominent broadcaster on radio stations such as **Capital Xtra** and **BBC Radio 1Xtra**. Her ability to connect with listeners and offer fascinating material has gained her plaudits and further reinforced her reputation as a multidimensional performer.

CHAPTER 6

Stand-up Comedy and Awards

London Hughes, a phenomenally brilliant stand-up comedian, has been tickling the funny bones of audiences for more than a decade. Her comic skills have graced some of the most known comedy festivals internationally, including the prestigious Edinburgh Fringe Festival, the Montreal Just For Laughs Festival, and the Melbourne International Comedy Festival.

What sets Hughes unique in the world of stand-up comedy is her unrepentant irreverence and her daring approach to confronting hard and sometimes sensitive issues, like race, gender, and sexuality. Her ability to handle these hard themes with humor and intelligence has gained her well-deserved accolades. London Hughes has a remarkable ability to connect with audiences, inviting them into her world, and offering her particular viewpoint on life.

Throughout her successful career, Hughes has won several prizes and honors, a tribute to her tremendous contributions to the comedy world. Notably, in 2017, she received the coveted Amused Moose Comedy Award at the Edinburgh Fringe Festival for her play **To Catch a Dick**, a testimony of her ability to generate comedy that connects with various audiences. Additionally, she has been nominated for various prizes, including the Chortle Award for Best Breakthrough Act and the Funny Women Award.

Beyond her stand-up humor, London Hughes has made significant appearances on several television series, films, and radio programs. Her flexibility as a performer goes beyond the stage, establishing her standing as one of the most dynamic and intriguing comedians in the business today.

CHAPTER 7

Personal Life and Philanthropy

London Hughes, noted for her comedy and wit on stage, has generally kept a discreet personal life, keeping many aspects out of the public view. However, she has offered snippets of her life growing up in southeast London and the hurdles she experienced while seeking a comedy career, bringing insight into her path.

In terms of philanthropic initiatives, London Hughes has provided her support to various humanitarian projects throughout the years, displaying her desire to have a good influence on the world. In 2019, she joined the Stand Up to Cancer charity event, an effort committed to collecting cash for critical cancer research and treatment.

Additionally, Hughes has been actively associated with Comic Relief, a prominent charitable organization fighting relentlessly to tackle poverty and social injustice on a worldwide basis.

Beyond her philanthropic activities, London Hughes has taken on the role of a mental health advocate, utilizing her platform as a comedian to focus awareness on crucial topics.

In an honest 2018 interview with The Guardian, she boldly disclosed her problems with anxiety disorder and earlier issues with depression. Her candor regarding mental health concerns acts as a light of hope and encouragement, pushing others to seek treatment when confronted with similar issues.

CONCLUSION

In the realm of comedy, where laughing is both an art form and a global language, London Hughes has emerged as a star. Her journey from the bustling streets of southeast London to the worldwide stages of stand-up comedy is a tribute to her skill, tenacity, and unflinching determination.

Throughout her storied career, London Hughes has captivated audiences with her irreverent humor, bold exploration of tough issues, and the distinct viewpoint she gives to the stage. From her groundbreaking work on the BBC Three comedy series **Laughter Shock** To her commanding presence at renowned comedy festivals like the

Edinburgh Fringe Festival, Montreal Just For Laughs Festival and Melbourne International Comedy Festival, she has left an indelible mark on the world of comedy.

Her ability to connect with audiences of various origins, ages, and walks of life is a credit to her humorous creativity. London Hughes has not only entertained but also questioned the current status quo, bravely diving into themes such as race, gender, and sexuality with comedy and insight. In doing so, she has pushed boundaries, destroyed preconceptions, and opened the way for a new generation of comedians to follow.

Beyond the laughing, London Hughes has embraced charity, utilizing her fame to assist philanthropic organizations such as

Stand Up to Cancer and Comic Relief. Her passion to raise awareness about mental health concerns has impacted many lives, bringing peace and support to others suffering their challenges.

As we reflect on London Hughes's life and work, it becomes obvious that she is more than a comedian; she is a pioneer, an advocate, and a beacon of humor and light in an often difficult world. Her influence stretches well beyond the bounds of the stage, pushing people to embrace their distinctive voices, face tough subjects with comedy, and have a good effect on the world.

In a world that sorely seeks comedy and connection, London Hughes has offered both in abundance. Her path is a monument to the transformational power of laughing, and her effect on the world of comedy is nothing short of legendary. As we flip the last page of this biography, we celebrate the life and career of London Hughes, a hilarious powerhouse who has permanently reshaped the landscape of comedy and left us all with a little more joy in our hearts.

Printed in Great Britain
by Amazon

28158770R00030